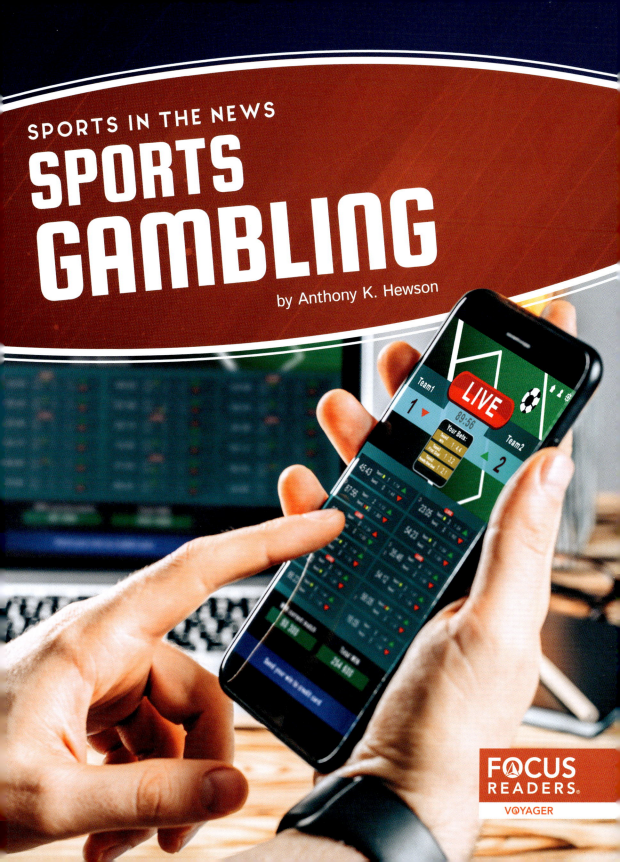

www.focusreaders.com

Copyright © 2021 by Focus Readers®, Lake Elmo, MN 55042. All rights reserved. No part of this book may be reproduced or utilized in any form or by any means without written permission from the publisher.

Focus Readers is distributed by North Star Editions:
sales@northstareditions.com | 888-417-0195

Produced for Focus Readers by Red Line Editorial.

Photographs ©: Shutterstock Images, cover, 1, 4–5, 41, 42–43; Mark J. Terrill/AP Images, 7; Cavan Images/Alamy, 8–9; Strobridge Lith. Co./Library of Congress, 11; Mary Altaffer/AP Images, 13; TSN/Icon SMI/Newscom, 14–15; Cincinnati Reds/MLB/Getty Images, 17; Rusty Kennedy/AP Images, 19; Everett Collection/Newscom, 21; Matt Rourke/AP Images, 22–23; David J. Phillip/AP Images, 25; Red Line Editorial, 27, 44; Julie Jacobson/AP Images, 28–29; John Locher/AP Images, 31; Alastair Grant/AP Images, 33; Gerry Broome/AP Images, 35; Louis Lanzano/AP Images, 36–37; David Stluka/AP Images, 39

Library of Congress Cataloging-in-Publication Data
Names: Hewson, Anthony K., author.
Title: Sports gambling / Anthony K. Hewson.
Description: Lake Elmo, Minn. : Focus Readers, [2021] | Series: Sports in the news | Includes index. | Audience: Grades 4-6
Identifiers: LCCN 2019054598 (print) | LCCN 2019054599 (ebook) | ISBN 9781644933930 (hardcover) | ISBN 9781644934692 (paperback) | ISBN 9781644936214 (pdf) | ISBN 9781644935453 (ebook)
Subjects: LCSH: Sports betting--Juvenile literature.
Classification: LCC GV717 .H48 2021 (print) | LCC GV717 (ebook) | DDC 796--dc23
LC record available at https://lccn.loc.gov/2019054598
LC ebook record available at https://lccn.loc.gov/2019054599

Printed in the United States of America
Mankato, MN
082020

ABOUT THE AUTHOR
Anthony K. Hewson is a freelance writer, originally from San Diego, who is now living in the Bay Area with his wife and their two dogs.

TABLE OF CONTENTS

CHAPTER 1
One Day in L.A. 5

CHAPTER 2
Off to the Races 9

CHAPTER 3
Major Scandals 15

CASE STUDY
"Shoeless" Joe Jackson 20

CHAPTER 4
How Sports Gambling Works 23

CHAPTER 5
Arguments for Sports Gambling 29

CASE STUDY
Adam Silver 34

CHAPTER 6
Arguments Against Sports Gambling 37

CHAPTER 7
The Future of Sports Gambling 43

Focus on Sports Gambling • 46
Glossary • 47
To Learn More • 48
Index • 48

CHAPTER 1

ONE DAY IN L.A.

May 31, 2002, was a great day for sports fans in Los Angeles. On a warm spring evening, horse racing fans were trying their luck at Hollywood Park. In the sixth race of the night, a horse named Osho was a **long shot**. She got a good start. Gradually, she caught up to the leaders. On the front stretch, she took the lead and pulled away. The crowd was delighted. The people who bet on Osho were delighted, at least.

Hollywood Park was open from 1938 to 2013.

Fans who picked the winning horse received a **payout** of $17.40 on a $2 bet.

A few miles to the north, the National Basketball Association (NBA) playoffs were in full swing. The Los Angeles Lakers faced the Sacramento Kings. The two teams were playing in Game 6 of the Western Conference Finals. The series had been incredibly exciting up to this point. But in Game 6, something seemed odd.

In the fourth quarter, the referees started calling more fouls than usual. And most of the fouls were on the Kings. The Lakers shot 27 free throws in the quarter. The Kings shot only nine. The Lakers went on to win the game.

Fans didn't know it at the time, but this game later became the center of a major **scandal**. Tim Donaghy was a referee in the game. In 2007, he admitted that he had bet on NBA games for years.

▲ Brian Shaw (left) of the Lakers attempts a shot during a 2002 playoff game.

The scandal showed just how easily a referee could change the outcome of a game. It shook public faith in the **integrity** of sports.

Gambling can add a fun experience for fans. But it also has a dark side that can affect the sports world in unexpected ways.

CHAPTER 2

OFF TO THE RACES

Gambling is nearly as old as civilization itself. The ancient Greeks played games of chance thousands of years ago. The ancient Romans played similar games. Even back then, gambling usually had a bad reputation. Many people considered it shameful to visit gambling houses.

Throughout history, gambling has often been regulated. For example, King Richard I of England created gambling regulations in the year 1190.

In ancient Rome, people often gambled on a game that was similar to checkers.

Other kings and queens in Europe also put limits on what types of games people could gamble on.

Horse racing was one of the earliest forms of sports gambling. The first horse racing track in America was built in New York in 1665. But gambling on horses was limited. For many years, only the horses' owners placed bets. They raised horses to see whose was faster.

Public horse tracks in the United States became popular in the 1800s. By 1890, the country had more than 300 tracks. However, **corruption** in horse racing nearly doomed the sport. The public was upset with fake **odds** and fake payouts. In response, many states banned all forms of betting. By 1910, only three states allowed gambling on horse racing. But even when gambling was illegal, people still took part in gambling on the side.

▲ A drawing from 1890 shows horses competing in a race.

Horse racing made a comeback in the 1930s. And the attitude toward gambling was starting to change. State governments saw an opportunity to tax gambling. These taxes would help state governments bring in more money. In the 1930s, 21 states opened new tracks.

The US government tried to regulate gambling as much as it could. Even so, illegal bets on sports continued to happen. Then in 1949, the state of Nevada legalized all sports gambling.

Bets outside Nevada were still illegal. But it was easy for people in other states to place bets with **bookmakers** in Nevada. Over time, however, the US government passed laws that made these activities illegal.

In 1992, the US government created the strictest law yet for sports gambling. The Professional and Amateur Sports Protection Act made nearly all sports gambling illegal. However, horse racing was not included in the ban. States that already had sports gambling, such as

➤ THINK ABOUT IT

When Nevada legalized sports gambling in 1949, the state had only 160,000 residents. By 1990, the state had more than one million residents. Do you think legalized sports gambling had any effect on the increase in population? Why or why not?

▲ Law enforcement officials discuss an online gambling ring in 2006.

Nevada, were allowed to keep it. But the law made sure sports gambling would not expand.

In the late 1990s and early 2000s, the rise of the internet made illegal gambling easier than ever before. The US government responded with more laws. In 2006, it passed the Unlawful Internet Gambling Enforcement Act.

Gambling was becoming more and more regulated. And the major North American sports leagues wanted to keep it that way. However, gambling fans hoped that would soon change.

CHAPTER 3

MAJOR SCANDALS

When US lawmakers decided to regulate sports gambling, they were influenced by major scandals. Such scandals were rare. But when they occurred, they convinced many people that sports gambling should be illegal.

The first game of the 1919 World Series ended with a shocking result. The Cincinnati Reds smoked the Chicago White Sox 9–1. The White Sox didn't play like the American League champs.

Members of the Chicago White Sox pose for a photo in 1919.

In the next game, Chicago looked just as rusty. Pitcher Claude "Lefty" Williams walked three batters in a row to give the Reds a win. The White Sox won the next three games. But the Reds ultimately won the series five games to three.

Several months later, evidence came to light. Some of the White Sox players had been **bribed** to intentionally lose the World Series. Professional gamblers had made the arrangements with the players. Then the gamblers bet heavily on the Reds, who they knew would win.

The players went to trial, but they were found not guilty. Some players had admitted their involvement. However, their statements were lost, and there was not enough evidence to convict them. Even so, eight members of the 1919 White Sox were banned from baseball for life. Today this incident is known as the Black Sox Scandal.

⚠ The Chicago White Sox and Cincinnati Reds compete in the 1919 World Series.

Major League Baseball (MLB) has a firm stance against gambling. It is even in the rule book. Rule 21 states that anyone who bets on baseball risks being banned from the game for life.

Decades after the Black Sox Scandal, Pete Rose became the center of another gambling case. Rose racked up more hits than anyone else in MLB history. He played most of his career with the Cincinnati Reds and later managed the club.

While serving as manager in 1989, evidence surfaced that Rose bet on baseball. He, too, was banned from the game for life. As a result, the sport's all-time hit king cannot be elected to the National Baseball Hall of Fame.

Baseball is far from the only sport that has had gambling scandals. In 1950, City College of New York (CCNY) had one of the best seasons in college basketball history. The Beavers were national champions. But a year later, it was revealed that some of the CCNY players were part of a plan to **fix** the results of games for illegal gamblers. In all, 32 players were convicted. It was

> ## THINK ABOUT IT
> Gamblers often do lots of research before deciding which bets to make. What kinds of information do you think they study? Why would that knowledge be helpful?

▲ Pete Rose dives toward third base during a 1981 game.

one of the biggest gambling scandals in college sports history.

These scandals identified one of the major risks of sports gambling. When huge amounts of money are involved, people may be tempted to break the rules. And that can cause fans to question the validity of the games' results.

CASE STUDY

"SHOELESS" JOE JACKSON

Joe Jackson was one of the 1919 White Sox players involved in the Black Sox Scandal. Jackson was one of the greatest players of his era. He had a batting average of .351 in 1919. Jackson had nothing to do with the planning of the scandal. First baseman Arnold "Chick" Gandil was in charge.

Gandil first offered his teammates $10,000 each to intentionally lose the series. Jackson refused. However, when Gandil increased the offer to $20,000, Jackson accepted. That was a huge amount of money at the time. It was three times the amount Jackson earned in a year.

Jackson still performed well in the series. He hit .375 and belted a home run. But he didn't have

Joe Jackson earned his nickname in 1908. A new pair of shoes hurt his feet, so he took them off during a game.

a single run batted in during the first five games. Chicago lost four of those games.

Baseball experts still debate Jackson's level of involvement. He did not take part in the planning. And there is no evidence that he did anything but try his best. Still, his bad judgment cost him his career. Jackson was banned from baseball for life. He almost certainly would have been a Hall of Famer. His lifetime batting average of .356 is still the third-best mark in MLB history.

CHAPTER 4

HOW SPORTS GAMBLING WORKS

Legal sports gambling is often run by casinos. These casinos have sportsbooks. Sportsbooks are places where people can bet on different sporting events. Typically, sportsbooks offer several kinds of bets. One of the simplest is called odds betting. This type of wager is common for individual sports, such as golf and boxing.

For example, suppose Rory McIlroy is playing in a golf tournament. His odds may be listed at 7–1.

Sportsbooks often have large screens so that gamblers can watch the games they bet on.

Now suppose a gambler bets $1 on McIlroy. If McIlroy wins, the gambler receives $7 plus the original $1. Most gamblers bet more than $1. Still, the percentages remain the same. A bet of $100 would pay $700 plus the original $100.

A second type of wager is known as a money line bet. This method is common when betting on team sports. For example, suppose the San Diego Padres are playing the Los Angeles Dodgers. The Padres are the **favorite**. They're listed at −120. If the Padres win, a gambler who bet $120 on the Padres would receive $100 plus the original $120. The Dodgers are the **underdog**. They're listed at +110. If the Dodgers win, a gambler who bet $100 on the Dodgers would receive $110 plus the original $100.

A third type of wager is called point spread betting. Suppose the Detroit Lions are playing the

⬆ At the beginning of the 2019 season, the Washington Nationals were listed at +2100 to win the World Series.

Chicago Bears. The Lions are favored to win by 4 points. This number is called the point spread. Now suppose a gambler bets $100 on the Lions. The gambler needs the Lions to cover the spread. That is, the gambler needs the Lions to win by 5 points or more. If that happens, the gambler wins $100 plus the original $100. If the Lions win by 3 points or fewer, the gambler loses her money.

25

A sportsbook sets its own numbers for each type of bet. Then, based on the outcome of the game, the sportsbook pays the winners. The sportsbook also keeps the losers' money.

Betting works differently in horse racing. This system is known as pari-mutuel betting. The term *pari-mutuel* comes from the French language. It means "betting among ourselves." That's because participants are not betting against a sportsbook. Instead, the odds are determined by how much money is bet on each horse.

Horses that receive the most bets are the favorites. The winning gamblers then receive a portion of the total amount that was bet on all the horses.

In horse racing, a horse can win (finish first), place (finish second), or show (finish third). If a gambler bets on a horse to win, he receives money only if the horse finishes first. But if a gambler bets on a horse to place, he receives money if the horse finishes first or second. However, the payout is much less. Similarly, if a gambler bets on a horse to show, he receives money if the horse finishes first, second, or third. But in that case, the payout is even lower.

HORSEPLAY

This table shows the payouts for a $2.00 bet at the 2019 Kentucky Derby. The winning horse, Country House, was a huge underdog at 65–1. On a $2.00 bet to win, the payout was $132.40.

Horse Name	Win	Place	Show
Country House	$132.40	$56.60	$24.60
Code of Honor	~	$15.20	$9.80
Tacitus	~	~	$5.60

CHAPTER 5

ARGUMENTS FOR SPORTS GAMBLING

The Professional and Amateur Sports Protection Act of 1992 made most sports gambling illegal in the United States. However, the law did not make gambling less popular. People still made bets illegally. Supporters of legalized gambling said the law was pointless. After all, people still found ways to make bets. Instead, supporters argued, sports gambling should be legal and regulated by the government.

Many people place illegal bets on the NCAA men's basketball tournament.

Gambling remained legal in certain states after 1992. In Nevada, for example, bookmakers operate behind the scenes. They make wagers on behalf of other people. All it takes is a phone call, and an out-of-state gambler can place a bet.

Many bookmakers are simply in the business of making bets. But some are involved with crime networks. And the money these bookmakers bring in can be used to fund more crime. If gambling were legal throughout the United States, those bookmakers would be out of business. As a result, crime could decrease.

State governments would also make more money if sports gambling were legal. Every time a gambler places a bet, the state would tax that bet. As a result, a gambling tax could bring in millions of dollars every year. The state could then use that money to pay for other projects.

▲ Gamblers place their bets at a sportsbook in Las Vegas.

Corruption has always been a major concern with sports gambling. With money on the line, anyone involved with a game could have something to gain. But supporters of legalized gambling argue that corruption is actually more likely if gambling remains illegal. If the government is watching, they argue, games will be harder to fix. Technology can track who makes bets and what they bet on. Officials can see if anything looks suspicious.

Supporters also argue that gambling makes watching sports more fun. If people have money on a game, they will be more interested. In Europe, fans can even make bets at games. For example, they can bet on the score at halftime. Or they can bet who is going to score next.

In this way, sports gambling is really no different than fantasy sports. Millions of people play fantasy sports each year. And people often gamble with their friends on the outcome of their fantasy seasons.

Daily fantasy sports leagues are similar to gambling. In these leagues, fans pay an entry fee.

➤ THINK ABOUT IT

Alcohol and guns can be dangerous if used improperly, but both are legal in the United States. Why do you think lawmakers have treated sports gambling differently?

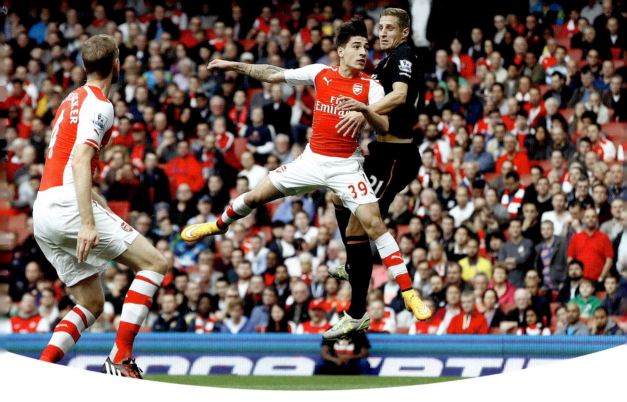

⚠ Soccer fans in England can easily place bets on their smartphones during games.

Then they set a lineup of players each day. If their players perform the best, they win money.

However, daily fantasy sports have been controversial. Some critics think they should be illegal like gambling. But the leagues are very popular. In total, fans win more than $2 billion each year. Legalized gambling would just be an extension of activities fans are already doing.

CASE STUDY

ADAM SILVER

The NBA knows all about the downside of sports gambling. The Tim Donaghy scandal rocked the league in 2007. David Stern was the league's commissioner at the time. He called it the worst situation an NBA commissioner had ever dealt with.

Adam Silver took over for Stern in 2014. Silver knew how much damage the Donaghy scandal had done to the NBA's reputation. And he knew the league had no way of detecting an illegal gambling ring.

Silver was not in favor of sports gambling at first. But he knew people were betting anyway. He thought the league had to be prepared to protect itself against scandals once betting became legal.

In 2014, Silver argued that laws needed to change. He said the US government should allow states to make sports gambling legal.

⚠ Adam Silver was the first commissioner of a major North American sports league to support legal gambling.

The leaders of other leagues have followed Silver's lead. Since 2014, the commissioners of MLB and the National Hockey League (NHL) announced partnerships with MGM Resorts. MGM is one of the largest operators of sportsbooks in the United States. Silver's early acceptance had opened up a new era of sports gambling.

CHAPTER 6

ARGUMENTS AGAINST SPORTS GAMBLING

Opponents of sports gambling have always had one major worry: corruption. People involved in a game may see an opportunity to make money. In exchange, they may be tempted to fix a game. As the Black Sox and Tim Donaghy scandals showed, these problems have existed for years.

With government oversight, professional sports might be safe from corruption. It would be difficult to fix a game without being caught.

Former NBA referee Tim Donaghy spent time in prison for his role in a game-fixing scandal.

But college sports are a different story. There are so many more athletes. And unlike the pros, college athletes don't get paid. The temptation to accept money in exchange for losing a game could be huge.

Currently, sportsbooks give odds for all sports, including college sports. So, even if fans aren't betting, they're aware of betting information. As a result, it can be difficult to separate the betting world from the sports world.

But there is more than just the integrity of games at stake. Legalized sports betting would make it easy for anyone to place a bet. Gambling can become an **addiction**, similar to drugs and alcohol. Some people are already addicted to gambling. Many more could become addicted if they had easier access to betting. Gambling addiction can have serious consequences. For

▲ The NCAA has more than 200 football teams in Division I and more than 150 teams in Division II.

instance, families can lose their savings and even their homes.

Opponents of sports gambling also point out that betting could actually be bad for fans. A fan may start out just wanting to bet on his favorite team to win. But the thrill of betting might be too much for him to stop. He could get caught up in the excitement. Over time, he may place larger bets and lose larger amounts of money.

And that is how the gambling industry thrives. The system is designed to make people lose.

Another argument against legalized gambling is that it won't raise as much money as some people claim. Even casinos make very little profit on sports gambling. New Jersey legalized sports gambling in the 1970s. State leaders estimated that a tax on gambling would pay for a wide variety of public services. But the gambling revenue has not been close to the state's estimates.

New Jersey residents have some of the highest tax rates in the United States. Even so, the state has often been short of money. Many people believed legalizing sports gambling would fix these issues, but it hasn't. New Jersey is a cautionary example for those who argue that gambling will solve a state's money problems.

▲ Sportsbooks need gamblers to lose, otherwise they won't make money.

Finally, opponents of gambling argue that it would change how people look at sports. Historically, sports have been independent of gambling. Once gambling starts, gambling and the sport become linked. Fans may never know if what they're watching is a legitimate result or if it is fixed for gambling purposes. If people want to gamble at a blackjack table in a casino, that is one thing. But opponents of gambling prefer it stays out of sports so there is less threat of corruption.

CHAPTER 7

THE FUTURE OF SPORTS GAMBLING

A breakthrough for sports gamblers came in 2018. That year, the US Supreme Court struck down the Professional and Amateur Sports Protection Act. The court's decision allowed states to decide for themselves whether sports gambling would be legal. By 2020, sports gambling was legal in more than one-quarter of the states. And many other states were working on bills to make it legal.

In many states, gamblers can place legal bets online.

In the United States, people wagered nearly $150 billion on sports in 2017. However, only 3 percent of that was legal. Through 2019, states were still struggling to capture revenue from gambling. For example, Rhode Island legalized sports gambling in November 2018. The state

> ## WHAT GAMBLERS BET ON

This chart shows the amount of money bet on various sports in Las Vegas from 1992 to 2018.

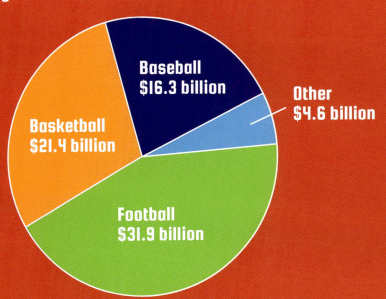

expected to take in more than $11 million in taxes during the first year. But three months after legalization, sports gambling had brought in only $150,000.

Even so, legal sports gambling was still very new. Supporters knew it would take time to gain acceptance. One thing that would help was the involvement of sports leagues. Over the years, the National Football League has opposed gambling. But the league has started investing in forms of gambling, such as daily fantasy sports.

With new laws and the support of pro leagues, sports gambling in the United States continued to gain support going into 2020. In addition, fears of corruption seemed to be decreasing over time. States still faced hurdles, such as how to regulate sports gambling properly. But legalized sports gambling appears to be here to stay.

FOCUS ON
SPORTS GAMBLING

Write your answers on a separate piece of paper.

1. Write a letter to a friend explaining what you learned about the Black Sox Scandal.

2. Do you think sports gambling should be legal? Why or why not?

3. If a gambler bets on a horse to show, where does the horse have to finish for the gambler to receive money?
   - **A.** It must finish first.
   - **B.** It must finish third.
   - **C.** It can finish first, second, or third.

4. Why did an increased number of fouls make it look like Game 6 of the 2002 Western Conference Finals was fixed?
   - **A.** The extra fouls showed that referees were trying to change the game's result.
   - **B.** The extra fouls showed that players were being more aggressive than usual.
   - **C.** The extra fouls showed that players were not trying hard enough to score.

Answer key on page 48.

GLOSSARY

addiction
A physical or mental need to keep doing something regularly.

bookmakers
People who make bets for other people.

bribed
Paid someone money to do something that person would otherwise not do.

corruption
Dishonest or illegal acts, especially by powerful people.

favorite
An individual or team that is expected to win.

fix
To illegally arrange a particular result.

integrity
Honesty, fairness, or trustworthiness.

long shot
A competitor that has a very small chance of winning.

odds
A measurement of how likely something is to happen.

payout
The amount a gambler receives if he or she wins a bet.

scandal
A disgraceful, controversial event.

underdog
An individual or team that is not expected to win.

TO LEARN MORE

BOOKS

Allen, John. *Addicted to Gambling*. San Diego: ReferencePoint Press, 2020.

Harris, Duchess, with Carla Mooney. *Fighting Stereotypes in Sports*. Minneapolis: Abdo Publishing, 2019.

McPherson, Stephanie Sammartino. *Doping in Sports: Winning at Any Cost?* Minneapolis: Lerner Publishing Group, 2016.

NOTE TO EDUCATORS

Visit **www.focusreaders.com** to find lesson plans, activities, links, and other resources related to this title.

INDEX

addiction, 38–39

Black Sox Scandal, 15–17, 20–21, 37

corruption, 10, 31, 37, 41, 45

Donaghy, Tim, 6, 34, 37

fantasy sports, 32–33, 45

fixing, 18, 31, 37, 41

horse racing, 5, 10–12, 26–27

Jackson, Joe, 20–21

Major League Baseball (MLB), 17, 21, 35

money line betting, 24

National Basketball Association (NBA), 6, 34

odds betting, 23–24

pari-mutuel betting, 26

point spread betting, 24–25

Professional and Amateur Sports Protection Act, 12, 29, 43

Rose, Pete, 17–18

Silver, Adam, 34–35

sportsbooks, 23, 26, 35, 38

Answer Key: 1. Answers will vary; 2. Answers will vary; 3. C; 4. A